FOCUS ON SAFETY

Be Aware of DANGER

BILL GUTMAN

Twenty-First Century Books
A Division of Henry Holt and Company/New York

For Cathy

Twenty-First Century Books
A Division of Henry Holt and Company, Inc.
115 West 18th Street
New York, NY 10011

Henry Holt® and colophon are trademarks of
Henry Holt and Company, Inc.
Publishers since 1866

Published in Canada by Fitzhenry & Whiteside Ltd.
195 Allstate Parkway, Markham, Ontario, L3R 4T8

Library of Congress Cataloging-in-Publication Data
Gutman, Bill.
Be aware of danger/Bill Gutman.—1st ed.
p.   cm.—(Focus on Safety)
Includes index.
Summary: Discusses how to deal safely with strangers
and dangerous situations in school and on the streets.
1. Safety education—Juvenile literature. 2. Children and strangers—
Juvenile literature. 3. Child abuse—Prevention—Juvenile literature.
[1. Strangers. 2. Crime prevention. 3. Safety.] I. Title.
II. Series: Gutman, Bill. Focus on Safety.
HQ770.7G87 1996   96-18617
613.6.—dc20   CIP
                                                                  AC

ISBN 0-8050-4142-7
First Editon—1996

Cover design by Robin Hoffman
Interior design by Kelly Soong

Printed in the United States of America
All first editions are printed on acid-free paper ∞.

1 3 5 7 9 10 8 6 5 4 2

Photo credits appear on page 80.

CONTENTS

FOREWORD

Safety is a simple six-letter word that means being secure and protected from harm. Everyone would like to feel safe, every day of their lives. That would be an ideal situation.

Unfortunately, none of us lives in a perfect world. In reality, this is a world where there are risks and where accidents and other bad things happen. And they can happen anywhere and at any time.

Many of the things that put us in jeopardy, however, can be avoided if we become more aware of our surroundings. All of us must be able to identify conditions that may put us in danger and take measures to alter those conditions. In other words, we must practice prevention.

For an overall focus on safety to really work, it must become a way of life, something each person is aware of every day. The safety net must always be up. No one wants to become just another statistic. And we should be willing to do everything in our power to keep that from happening.

INTRODUCTION

Growing up today isn't easy. In a way, it never was. Children have always had to go through a number of difficult stages as they began school, grew to their teens, then became young adults, and finally adults. But in today's world, the potential for violence and danger outside the home can sometimes seem overwhelming.

A recent survey by Child Trends, an organization doing research for the Foundation for Child Development, showed that 68 percent of children of various ages feared an intruder might enter their homes. Some 28 percent of those asked said they feared violence outside the home. Those fears are not unfounded.

The National Education Association (NEA) says that in the United States, more than 135,000 children leave for school every day carrying a handgun. Many more carry a knife or other weapon. In addition, the survey also says that some 160,000 children stay home from school each day because they fear they will be intimidated, attacked, or injured in some way.

When asked, nearly 50 percent of children say they have been bothered by adults or other children while playing outdoors. Of these, 43 percent report being harassed by older children. One third have been threatened with a beating, while 12 percent report actually having been beaten up. Nearly 25 percent have had personal property taken from them, while 5 percent report having been robbed of money.

Other children fear being abducted by a stranger who may want to sexually abuse them. It sounds like an almost hopeless situation. Once thought of as a problem confined to poor sections of big cities, crime and street danger have spread to the suburbs and even to rural America. Though there is a higher risk in some areas than others, nearly all children must be made aware of the possibility of danger when they walk the streets, take public transportation, use public facilities, are part of large crowds, or simply attend school. It is up to today's kids (as well as their parents and guardians) to learn about potential danger outside the home and to prepare themselves for it. By being aware of danger, you can often avoid it. And if you are caught in a dangerous situation that cannot be avoided, you can often lessen your personal risk simply by being prepared to face it.

Violence on the streets and in schools, especially in areas where it isn't a common occurrence, is still shocking to many people. At a high school in New York State's Dutchess County, about 60 miles north of New York City, the first day of the 1995–1996 school year brought a near tragedy. A student entered the school and immediately began slashing another with two knives. It wasn't a fatal attack, but it could have been.

Police felt the incident stemmed from something that happened between the two during the summer. It had spilled over into the school. This was not an inner-city school. It was a suburban school in a picturesque setting. Yet it was a school where problems had occurred before, from fires set intentionally during the school day to incidents caused by racial prejudice.

If you surveyed other schools, you would find similar incidents occurring across the country. And they take place not only in the schools but on the streets, at dances and concerts, and any other place where large numbers of kids gather.

Unfortunately, there is nothing that will eliminate these incidents entirely. That's why being prepared and knowing what to do when confronted by a dangerous situation is more important now than ever before.

DEALING WITH FEAR

The dictionary defines *fear* as anxiety caused by real or possible danger. Everyone has fears. Most people try to understand their fears, then control them. Some fears are more immediate than others. If someone fears losing his job, he may work harder to protect himself from being fired. His fear may be real or imagined.

But if someone walking through a dark parking lot each night fears being mugged, that fear is immediate. The danger may become real at any time without warning. It's more difficult to deal with that immediate fear, which is there each time that person enters that parking lot.

It's often much more difficult for youngsters to deal with fear than it is for adults. That doesn't mean children's fears are any more or less real than adults' are. But, for children, fears are relatively new and are more difficult to understand. Children are, by their nature, innocent. If young children are taught to be nice, and that the world is nice, it can be tremendously difficult for them to understand that *not everything is nice*. When a youngster experiences fear for the first time, it can be very difficult to deal with.

Physical violence is the biggest fear that most youngsters experience. Not only are kids exposed to violence many times over on television, but some see it on the streets at a very young age. This street violence often involves older kids. Surveys have shown that kids go after other kids even more than they target the elderly, who often can't defend themselves.

It is the young who are the most frequent victims of violent crimes, such as robbery and assault. According to a study conducted by Child Trends, the biggest object of fear of one in every five youngsters is another young person in the neighborhood or at his school who has assaulted or threatened to assault him.

FACING UP TO FEAR

Dealing with your fears is the first step toward dealing with dangers outside the home in a positive way. Only when you understand your fears and control them can you learn how to deal with danger. Once you face up to your fears, you can learn how to protect yourself. You will be more confident about dealing with the world outside your home and family. That doesn't mean your fears will disappear. Some degree of fear can work for you, because it will cause you to keep your guard up and not get careless.

How do you control your fears? The first important thing is to talk about them. The best people to talk with are your parents or guardians, or another trusted adult—an aunt or uncle, a teacher, a law enforcement officer. Sure, you can also talk to your friends. But in most cases, an understanding adult can give you better advice. Friends can sometimes make the fears worse.

In today's world, even young children have some awareness of danger. Even if they haven't been victims themselves, they hear about violence and danger from friends or older brothers or sisters and see a great deal of it on television, either on the news or on prime-time shows. Evidence shows that kids think about fear very often and from an early age.

Children who have been warned about small things—like looking both ways before they cross the street—from a young age will more readily accept warnings about keeping themselves

Police officers often visit schools to speak about safety issues. If you have questions, ask them!

safe from greater dangers. Those who come from families where people rarely talk, or where children are *scolded* after a small accident happens, may have more difficulty talking about their fears, understanding warnings, and protecting themselves.

If your parents or guardians don't seem to want to talk with you about your fears, tell them how important the subject is to you. However, if you find that the adults in your family simply can't handle these kinds of discussions, then it's time to talk with another adult.

When talking to an adult about a fear, watch his reaction. Does he remain calm? Does he acknowledge that your fear is very real and must be handled? Or does he get excited and tell you you are making a mountain of a molehill? Does he dismiss you by saying there's nothing to worry about? Does he make you feel ashamed or babyish because you have the fear?

If you get only negative reactions you *must* seek out another adult. Fears—real or imagined—must be handled quickly and in an intelligent manner. Some adults still feel that by making light of a child's fear, it will go away. But those adults are not living in a child's world. They don't look up at adults on the street and wonder if they might be dragged into a car and kidnapped. Adults don't have to face walking toward three or four bigger kids wondering if it's best to cross the street or turn and run in order to avoid being mugged or robbed.

There was a time when many parents and guardians taught their children to be polite and courteous, to show respect to all adults, and always do the right thing. That, they said, would keep kids safe. Unfortunately, it simply doesn't work that way anymore. And a child who is told he is perfectly safe on the streets can lose all his trust in the adult world if he finds out the hard way that he isn't.

Fears, as well as the dangers that create them, must be openly discussed between kids and the adults who care for them. It must be acknowledged that there is a basis for those fears in today's world. You need to know that there are bad people who might try to harm you, and to understand some of the reasons why this is so. Only then will you also understand that you must learn the best ways to avoid harm. This might mean not always following the rules of being a nice, good person. But if you understand that you need to be aware of danger in order to protect yourself from it, you'll be on the right track toward facing up to your fears.

Today there are many organized groups that help children deal with their fears and cope with the dangers they find outside their homes. These groups may be organized by your school, your church, your local police department, or simply by adults in your community. Working with one of these groups will help you to realize that you are not alone. Lots of kids have fears, and lots of adults want to help them learn how to handle them.

WHEN TO BREAK THE GOLDEN RULE

A good kid is a nice kid. That's been a general rule for many years.

Joey is such a nice young boy.

Melissa is a lovely girl, so polite all the time.

These are among the compliments parents and guardians most like to hear about their kids. It makes them feel they have done a good job raising their children.

Do unto others as you would have them do unto you.

This is another rule adults have taught to generations of children. But in the world we live in today, the golden rule does not always apply.

It's often difficult for parents and guardians to teach kids not to be nice. But knowing when not to be polite is one of the most important things to learn if you are going to protect yourself outside your home. Being nice to everybody all the time can often lead to danger.

What are some of the rules that will sometimes have to be broken? Here are a few things you *can't* always do on the streets. You can't:

1. Always listen to an adult and do what they ask.
2. Always be polite to an adult (or anyone) when they ask you a question or ask for a favor.
3. Always accept an offer of help with gratitude.

4. Always give a polite, honest answer to a question, especially when asked by an adult.

There are times when being nice isn't the right thing to do. Politeness, honesty, compliance, and trust do not always apply when you are away from your home and family.

On the streets, you should be prepared *not* to listen to strangers. You should *not* answer any personal questions. You should *ignore* offers of a ride, a free movie, or food. You should *not* be polite and courteous if a stranger strikes up a conversation with you. You should *not* help someone you don't know, no matter how critical the situation seems. (If you feel you must help, the best thing for you to do is run and get an adult!)

These are just some of the ways you must learn to keep your guard up on the street. Now let's see how these new rules apply to certain specific situations. It can be really difficult to know when to put your personal safety first. But remember this: you have every right to protect yourself when any situation makes you feel threatened.

3

MAKE YOURSELF
STREET SMART

According to Ed Muir, head of School Safety for the United Federation of Teachers in New York City, kids begin running into trouble at about age eleven. This is when most children start to demand more freedom. They also tend to begin going outside of their own neighborhoods and move on to middle school and then high school. So they are away from their family more often, and traveling new streets and unfamiliar neighborhoods.

No one can really predict who will get into trouble on the street. Sometimes a person is simply in the wrong place at the wrong time. No amount of street smarts or training can change that. But there are a number of things you can do to lower your risk of danger on the street and increase your odds of staying safe.

Which kids are most likely to run into trouble? There is a term for people who look like easy victims: *looking muggable*. The things that make for an easy, muggable target have been pointed out by convicted muggers themselves, who have cooperated with authorities to describe the kinds of people they would go after if they were planning a mugging or a robbery.

For starters, you should not go out on the street *looking rich*. Even if you come from a wealthy family, don't flaunt your ability to look better than your peers. Wearing the latest in athletic wear—jackets with team logos, high-priced sneakers named for a National Basketball Association superstar—attracts other kids who can't afford these items. They may decide to simply mug you and take them.

Even expensive clothing that might not be considered "cool" on the street will still mark you as someone who might be carrying a substantial amount of money. Again, what you wear can make you a target. Any items of clothing that are expensive-looking, flashy, or desirable on the street can mark you for danger.

It's best to wear clothes that make you look like just one of the crowd. Carrying expensive items such as walkmans or boom boxes can also make you ripe for a robbery. Leave these things at home. Don't parade down the street showing them to everyone. You're only asking for trouble if you do.

WATCH YOUR BODY LANGUAGE

It isn't only what you wear and carry on the street that could lead to trouble. It's also how you walk and how you act. Your body language can make you appear muggable. The number-one rule of street safety is to be alert.

Muggers, both old and young, look for people who appear to be in a daze, or unhappy, or unaware. These people don't have a confident and alert look. They are not watching what is happening around them. Or they might have a timid, worried look, constantly glancing back over their shoulders in a nervous manner.

Experts say that you should walk down the street in a way that demonstrates confidence and alertness. Walk briskly, with your head up. Stay focused on things going on around you. Instead of worried looks, just move your eyes around as if you are casually checking things out. Walk with a purpose, as if you know exactly where you are going, even if you don't. If you seem confused or lost, or act as if you're in unfamiliar sur-roundings, troublemakers can pick up those signals.

*Carrying an expensive item, like a boom box,
can make you a target for robbery.*

Your body language doesn't have to make you look tough or ready to fight, but it should make you appear like someone who knows what is going on around you. That will make muggers or bullies less likely to pick on you when they are looking for trouble.

SIZING UP SITUATIONS

The right dress and body language are two things that can help keep you safe on the street. Your own ability to size up certain situations can also help. How to handle various situations you run into when you are away from home is something you can learn from your own experience; from parents, guardians, or friends; or from someone who has already developed street smarts. And sometimes your own instincts will tell you what to do. Learn to trust your instincts. If you feel threatened, or afraid, do something about it. Don't ignore those feelings. Crime victims often say things like "I knew I shouldn't go down that alley," or "Something at that playground just didn't feel right." They didn't heed their instincts until it was too late.

One rule is to avoid getting cornered by a group, whether they are your own age or older. If you are walking down the street and see a group of kids walking toward you or hanging out on the corner, you've got to size up the situation quickly. If they appear tough or unruly, or seem to be shouting at people and possibly looking for trouble, then cross the street.

Don't make it look as if you are running away. Keep walking confidently as if you are simply continuing to move to your destination.

If there are only a couple of kids on the corner and the street is busy with many people walking back and forth, then it probably isn't necessary to cross the street. Just keep walking past them in your usual manner. But as in any situation where there is potential danger, follow your gut instincts. If your instincts tell you to cross the street, then cross.

It's also important to size up situations in certain types of public places. If you want to use a public rest room, it's always

*If you find yourself in an unfamiliar
neighborhood, walk confidently.
Showing nervousness or confusion
can make you vulnerable.*

best to go with a friend. This is especially true if the rest room appears deserted or if there is just one person inside. Crowded or heavily trafficked public rest rooms are safer. And always remember to keep packages or purses safe while you use a rest room. If you can leave your things with a friend, that's best. If not, don't put them in a place where they can be snatched. Keep parcels and purses close to you and up off the floor.

Be especially careful when you are in unfamiliar neighborhoods. When you don't know the territory, you can often look like an easier target because your body language gives you away. You are also less likely to know the safe places, where you can get help, and whom you can trust.

In unfamiliar places, all the usual safety rules apply. Walk in the middle of the sidewalk. Never walk close to buildings—where you pass doorways and alleys—or near bushes that can conceal a mugger. Avoid deserted areas, such as empty parking lots, deserted alleyways, empty buildings. Even in your own neighborhood, a shortcut you take with your friends on the way to school should be avoided if it's dark, or if you are alone.

In any potentially dangerous situation, there is always safety in numbers. Where there is a concentration of people, there is generally less danger. When there are a lot of people around, you are also more likely to find police officers, security guards, or other adults who can help if you need it. Even just being with a bunch of kids is safer than being alone. So whenever possible, avoid dangerous situations and stay where the people are.

WHAT NOT TO CARRY

There are times when everyone has to take something valuable with them to school, to a party, or to a friend's house. Or maybe you just bought something and you need to carry it home from the store. In any case, whenever you are carrying a valuable piece of merchandise out in the open on the street you become more of a target for a robbery.

If you must carry something valuable, try to conceal its identity as much as possible. Put it in a bag or a box, or wrap it in plain paper. A potential robber seeing that you are carrying a new compact disc player may come after it. But if he sees you carrying an unmarked box, with no way of knowing the contents, he may not bother.

As a rule, the less you advertise what you're carrying, the less likely it is that someone will try to take it from you. If you have to take something fairly large and costly somewhere, see if an adult can drive you. That is the safest way.

In addition to large items that can't be concealed, there are some other things you shouldn't carry when you're out on the streets. Unless absolutely necessary, never carry large sums of money. There is always the chance of a mugging or robbery. As a general rule, never carry more money than you can afford to lose.

If for some reason you do have a large amount of money with you, never flash all of it in a public place. If you need one dollar, don't take out a roll of bills to peel it off. If your money is in a wallet, don't open it in front of another person who can see there are a number of bills inside.

You should also avoid wearing any kind of flashy or expensive jewelry—rings, watches, earrings, bracelets. In addition, you shouldn't flash other small items that are often the target of thieves, such as bus passes, small radios or walkmans, cameras, or even collectible sports cards. The less you show in public, the better. And if you fear something valuable might be taken, don't carry it. Better to be safe than sorry.

THINGS YOU SHOULD CARRY

Most kids always carry some keys and a wallet or purse when they leave the house. The wallet or purse usually contains some kind of identification with a name and street address on it. Always keep your keys separate from your wallet or purse. That way, chances are you won't lose both at once. If you lose a purse or wallet with keys in it, the person finding it will have both your address and the keys with which to enter your house.

In addition to the money you need for the day, it's also a good idea to carry a small amount of emergency money for either a ride on public transportation (a bus, subway, cab) or at least for a phone call. This money should always be hidden where a quick-striking mugger won't find it. This way, if your wallet or purse is stolen, you'll still be able to get home safely, or to call someone for a ride. And if you forget to carry the emergency money, or lose it, or if the mugger manages to get it, keep this in mind: many pay phones today give you a dial tone without putting money in, enabling you to make a collect call.

There are some experts who feel that all kids should carry what is called *mugging money*. The theory is that some muggers will be satisfied if you give them a few dollars. But if you have nothing, they might become infuriated and assault you. But you never know when a mugger or muggers might feel the mugging money isn't all you have. Again, if muggers feel you are holding out, they may become violent as well.

So whether or not you should carry mugging money is up to you and your family. It might also be a good idea to get the opinions of some experts in your area—law enforcement officers or counselors who specialize in analyzing street crime.

There is one thing that you should never carry. That is a weapon—a gun, a knife, a disabling spray such as mace, a stun gun, or anything that can cause serious injury or worse to either a mugger or to yourself. First of all, the weapon may be illegal in your area. By carrying an illegal weapon, you are breaking the law. Second, by trying to defend yourself with a weapon, you may be the one who gets hurt. Or, if you injure, disable, or perhaps kill a mugger, you could be brought up on serious criminal charges and your family may face a potentially expensive lawsuit.

A better idea might be to carry what is called a personal safety alarm. This is a battery-operated device that emits a loud, piercing sound. The sound won't stop until the battery dies, and will often frighten a mugger, robber, or molester who doesn't want to attract attention. Some of these alarms can be worn on your belt or in another convenient place so they can be switched on quickly. Also, if you wear the alarm on your belt, a potential mugger may see it and decide to look for another victim who doesn't have the alarm.

Some people still suggest the old-fashioned whistle as an alarm. But if you are grabbed from behind, you probably won't have time to put a whistle in your mouth to blow it. And it can be knocked away quickly. The personal alarm can be switched on instantly and cannot be switched off.

WHAT TO DO IF YOU FEEL THREATENED

If you are in a situation where you feel a person or group of persons is following you or about to mug you, there are several things you can do to avoid a possible confrontation. As mentioned earlier, one of the first things you can do is cross the street. If the person you want to avoid crosses as well, he may well be following you.

If you are in the middle of a town or city, you should then go into the nearest store. Tell the clerk or owner of your fear and ask to use the phone. Call a family member or a friend and ask them to come pick you up. If you can't reach anyone, call the police. Don't go back outside, especially if the person who was following you is still lurking about.

If you are in a suburban or rural neighborhood and think you're being followed, go to the nearest house and ask to use the phone. Or, if you know the owner of the house, ask for a ride home. If you have left one place and are heading for another, with no store or house in between, then you must decide how to reach safety quickly. If you aren't halfway to your destination, turn and go back to the place you just left. If you are more than halfway, continue. If necessary, run.

Another safety tip is to look for landmarks or places to go to if you are followed as you go about your daily business. Always be aware how far you are from the last safe building or the next one on your route. In other words, always have in mind a place you can go to quickly if you must. Think about these things on an ordinary day, when you are calm. When you are scared, afraid that someone is following you, you may not be able to think clearly. Yet that is the very time you must act quickly. By planning ahead, you may be able to protect yourself in time of trouble.

If you feel someone is following you in a car, then turn around and go back the other way. That way, the car will have to make a U-turn to keep following you. If the car turns, look for the nearest store or house. Or, if you can, move quickly to an area that is crowded.

A good way of seeking safety is to look for someone in a uniform. It doesn't have to be a police officer. It can be a firefighter, a letter carrier, even a delivery person. Many companies tell their employees to help children whenever possible.

Besides being followed, there are some other ways trouble may begin. Assailants often test their potential victims to find which will be the easiest target. Muggers and even bullies will sometimes bump you, push you, or block your way. They often want to see how you react.

When these things happen the best advice is to just move away quickly. Try not to show fear or any expression in your face. This kind of body language will make you appear alert and in control. An expressionless, almost stony face can actually hide your fears. Some experts even suggest practicing this kind of "street face" in front of a mirror.

If anyone begins to hassle you verbally, making wise re-marks or even threats, use the same formula. Ignore them and move away quickly, almost as if you are bored with the entire sit-uation. Don't try to answer back, ask to be left alone, or make a threat in return. That usually doesn't work.

DON'T SAY A WORD

If you find yourself threatened by someone who seems intent on mugging or robbing you, talking to the assailant can some-times make things worse. The mugger hopes to take what he wants and get away quickly. Talking will slow him down. And it may make him angry as well.

If you are asked for money and answer with a firm *no*, you may be setting up a confrontation. You should also not make reference to what is actually happening. In other words, don't say, "Why are you robbing [or mugging] me? I have no money."

Above all, don't try to talk tough. That becomes a challenge. And don't trade insults or racial slurs with someone you think might want to rob or mug you. That, too, will encourage a con-frontation. At the same time, don't plead or beg to be left alone. That's a sign of weakness that makes the mugger (usually also a bully) feel even more powerful.

WHAT TO DO IF YOU ARE MUGGED

Most muggers want to work fast. They want to get what they're after and get away quickly. Street muggings have often been called "grab and run" crimes. The mugger is not looking for a fight.

If a kid comes up to you and demands money or threatens to beat you up, it's better to hand something over than risk the physical injury. Police officials will tell you that neither money nor possessions are worth getting injured or killed for. Some kids, especially boys, feel the manly or "macho" thing to do is fight back. There are too many variables to consider to give definite advice here. Is it one against one or three against one? Is the attacker bigger and older? Does he have a weapon? Does the attacker have friends waiting nearby?

All these questions must be answered in an instant if you make a decision to fight. Sometimes that simply is not possible. So the rule of thumb is not to fight unless it is a last resort to protect yourself. In most cases you are better off giving the attacker what he wants and trying to get away from the scene as quickly as possible.

If you find yourself being physically attacked, the natural thing is to call for help. But experts say it's better to yell *"Fire!"* than *"Help!"* There is more chance that people will come to investigate a fire than to help in an assault. The attacker might have a weapon, and many people don't want to put their own safety and perhaps their lives at risk.

During a mugging, keep your wits about you. Try to remember what the attacker looked like. Then go right to the police and report it. An assault or a robbery is a crime. The police should know about it. Muggers are usually repeat offenders. They continue to mug and rob to get money and possessions. If the police know enough about a mugger, even if they gather that information from several victims, they may be able to get the mugger off the street. So, always report a mugging to the police. Let them decide how important the information you give them is. By talking with the police, you may be able to prevent someone else from being mugged.

WHAT ABOUT AFTERWARD?

It isn't easy for children to deal with being mugged, robbed, or assaulted. Both the very young and older kids (into their teens) often feel embarrassed and humiliated after they become victims. They often have a sense of helplessness, as if their personal lives have been violated. Kids often blame themselves for what happened. They feel they should have done something

MEET MCGRUFF

In 1982, McGruff the Crime Dog became a symbol for one of the most successful programs in the nation designed to help people in distress. The program began with an agreement between Utah Hands Up (now the Utah Council for Crime Prevention) and the National Crime Prevention Council to use McGruff as a "block home" symbol.

Over the next five years, the McGruff House idea and its organizational procedures spread to communities across the nation. In a nutshell, McGruff Houses are used as temporary havens for children and adults who find themselves in an emergency or frightening situation.

These situations may include being bullied, followed, lost, or hurt while walking in a neighborhood. A McGruff House is not used as a place to get a drink of water, to use the telephone or the bathroom. It's for people in serious situations. The McGruff House program has now spread to nearly 600 communities, with more than 1,000 operational neighborhood programs managing more than 100,000 volunteer McGruff Houses.

The program's recognition factor is incredible. According to statistics compiled at the National McGruff House Network headquarters in Salt Lake City, Utah, 99 percent of children aged nine to twelve are aware of McGruff. Some 96 percent of teenagers also know about the program, as do 72 percent of adults.

more to protect themselves. Or they feel they should have been smart enough to avoid the incident.

In truth, kids should not take the blame if they are mugged, robbed, or assaulted on the street. It's up to parents, guardians, or other adults to understand this and make sure children do

And a full 100 percent of crime prevention personnel interviewed said they were aware of McGruff.

But the safe houses aren't all. In 1986, the McGruff Truck Program was also begun in Utah. It started with the Mountain Fuel Supply Company in Salt Lake City and has now spread to fifty-eight companies throughout the United States. These companies put the McGruff Crime Dog symbol on their utility trucks.

The goal of the McGruff Truck Program is to make neighborhoods safer for children. Drivers are trained to call for appropriate help when flagged down by a child or individual in distress. All trucks in the program must have two-way radios.

Drivers stop and respond to children in distress. A driver finds out what the problem is, reassures the child, then calls his company's dispatcher and describes the situation. The driver stays with the child until help arrives. Last of all, he fills out a McGruff Truck incident report, which is put on file.

Both the McGruff House and McGruff Truck programs have been extremely successful. Executive Director Tibby Milne was honored by President George Bush and the National Office, Victims of Crime for developing a program which has significantly contributed to the prevention of victimization of children.

The next time you see the McGruff slogan, "Take a Bite Out of Crime," remember this: it works.

not feel guilty. If you have been a victim and feel guilty about it, speak to your parents or guardians. If you feel they don't understand or haven't been much help, make arrangements to speak to another adult. It might be a law enforcement officer, a clergyman, or a counselor who specializes in such cases.

Even if you didn't follow all the rules of street safety, do not feel guilty if you were a victim. You didn't create muggers or bullies. Maybe you just weren't as careful as you should have been. But you didn't cause the incident to happen. The mugger did. Remember that the attacker committed a crime and intended to commit a crime. Being a victim is not a crime. Don't blame yourself. But do learn from the incident and try your best to protect yourself in the future.

PUBLIC TRANSPORTATION AND PUBLIC PLACES

Time spent getting from here to there means time around traffic—cars, trucks, and buses. Traffic represents more of a potential danger in cities than in the suburbs. But failure to follow basic rules can get anyone in trouble anywhere.

Most kids learn the rules of safely moving in and around traffic early, whether they live in the city or the country. Cross at the green, not in between. Look both ways before crossing. Don't play in traffic. Don't walk out onto the street between parked cars or from behind a bush or tree. If there are no sidewalks and you must walk on the side of the road, walk on the left facing oncoming traffic. If you're on a bike, a skateboard, or in-line skates, don't grab on to a moving vehicle for a free ride.

Despite these rules, which are so obvious that they may strike you as being silly, there are numerous accidents and tragedies involving children and motor vehicles each year. You only have to read your local newspaper every day and you'll see how often it happens. Many, perhaps most, of these accidents can be prevented simply by following the rules.

But in addition to the basic rules of safety, the number-one rule of the street also applies. *Stay alert!* And never assume that a driver is going to obey traffic laws to the letter. On the contrary, assume he won't. Just by being aware, you may save yourself from being hit by a driver running a red light or a stop sign.

GETTING WHERE YOU'RE GOING

The use of public transportation should not put young people in danger. Unfortunately, in today's world it sometimes can. Even in suburban and rural areas, safety problems connected with public transportation may exist.

Many kids use public transportation to go to and from school, so these safety issues cannot be ignored. There are some basic rules you should always observe in order to stay safe:

1. **Don't get too close.** Never stand too close to the edge of the platform when waiting for a subway or a train. There have been incidents when deranged people have pushed someone under the wheels of an oncoming train. In the subway, someone could reach out from between the cars and try to grab your purse or jewelry. This could result in a serious injury or worse.

   The same rule applies at a bus stop. Don't get too close as the bus pulls in. You could be pushed or accidentally bumped or jostled into the path of the vehicle.

   It's no different at school-bus stops in rural areas. At certain times of the year in part of the country, kids are picked up early in the morning when it's still dark or just getting light. So don't get too close to the road. Drivers of automobiles may not see you. And once you're on the bus, obey the rules the driver has set down. These rules are for your protection and the driver's.

2. **Stay away from isolated train and bus stations.** Train or bus stations with very few people can be an ideal place for those with bad intentions to lurk. Unless you have a large group of friends with you, stay away from these isolated stations. Plan to travel during a busier time of day, or use a different route.

   If there are people waiting at a station, stand near them. Don't wait off by yourself. Don't isolate yourself so you can be cut off and trapped. Remember, there is safety in numbers.

3. **Don't flash money.** Same rules as on the street. Have just the

*Don't assume that school-bus safety is
only your driver's responsibility. You can play a
part in it, too, by paying attention to what's
going on around you, and by following the rules.*

money you need for your fare in your hand. Don't pull out a roll of bills or open a wallet or purse for others to see.

4. **Stay close to someone in authority.** If the train or bus is not crowded, try to take a seat close to the driver or conductor. A lot of kids like to ride in the back of a bus or train, but that may not be the safest place to be if trouble starts. Don't sit by yourself or in an isolated spot. If someone that you don't trust sits near you, move away. If you still feel you are in danger, get off. But only get off at a stop where there are other people—never at an isolated or dark stop.

5. **Move away if you are bumped or bothered.** Someone who picks you as a target on a crowded bus or train, may start to bump and jostle you. Some men will take this opportunity to grab at a woman or child, sometimes touching their private parts, using the crowded conditions as an excuse. Some people react to this kind of situation by freezing. This is a reaction of shock caused by something that is unexpected and unpleasant. It is usually the reaction of someone who hasn't experienced this kind of harassment before, often a young person.

   What you should do is move away immediately. Then tell the driver or a conductor what has just happened. If it is so crowded that you can't move away quickly, you might try shouting, "Don't touch me!" Or "Keep your hands off me!" Drawing attention to whoever is bothering you is often enough to make them stop. These people don't want to be noticed, and they certainly don't want to be arrested. Just make sure the person doesn't follow you when you get off the bus or train. If he does, you know what to do. Follow the instructions in Chapter Three.

6. **Make sure you know how to get home safely if you miss your school bus.** Almost every kid who takes a school bus has missed it once or twice. Plan ahead so you'll know what to do if this happens to you.

   Likewise, think about what to do if you miss your stop on the school bus, bus, or train. You may end up in an unfamiliar area, and you'll need to be able to get home safely.

PUBLIC PLACES AND LARGE GATHERINGS

Kids have always liked to gather in popular public places. Whether it be a shopping mall, an arcade, a rock concert, a dance, or a sporting event, kids like to go where there are other kids. But there may also be older kids and possibly some adults there as well. And some of these people may be looking for trouble. Both kids and their parents or guardians should be very aware of the kinds of people likely to be found at public places and events.

If you and your parents or guardians agree that you can go to a sports arena or a concert, there are certain precautions you should take. To begin with, never go alone. It's best to go with several friends and for all of you to stay together. Never allow yourself to be separated from your friends in a place where you might be cornered by someone looking to rob or mug you. Remember to hold on to your ticket stub, even after you have reached your seat. If you should leave your seat, your ticket stub can help you find your way back if you get confused. The ticket stub also proves you are sitting in the right seat if you should be challenged by an usher or security guard.

If you are going to a mall, a movie, or even a concert at night, you should be driven and picked up by adults if at all possible. Don't walk or take public transportation late at night. It's just not a good idea. You might be embarrassed about needing a ride. But that's a small price to pay for staying safe.

When you are out in public, always be aware of what is going on around you. Try to stay close to authority figures, whether it be a police officer, a shop owner, a mall security guard, or an usher at a movie or concert. If you can't see them, know where they can be found quickly. Then, if you begin having problems with an older kid or an adult, you'll know where to go for help.

Another good tip is to never take anything to eat or drink from any stranger who wants to simply *give* it to you. Even if you

WHAT TO DO IF GUNFIRE BREAKS OUT NEAR YOU

To be in an area where gunfire breaks out can be frightening. It can also be deadly. Numerous innocent people are killed or wounded by stray bullets each year. With so many illegal handguns on the streets, the possibility of being caught in the middle of a shoot-out isn't so far-fetched. This is especially true in certain areas of big cities where crime is prevalent and drug deals go down regularly.

Rule number one is to avoid these high-risk areas whenever possible. Instead of passing through a neighborhood where shoot-outs occur, try to find an alternate route around it. It might take you longer to reach your destination, but it will be safer.

A loud explosion usually does not indicate a gunshot. A gunshot is more of a popping sound since the guns generally used on the streets are handguns. If you are on the street and hear these popping sounds, take cover immediately.

You can get under something, like a nearby car. Just make sure it isn't a car that is about to pull out. If there is a doorway within 10 to 20 feet of you, make a dash for it. You are always safer in a doorway, a hallway, or inside a building. But if that doorway is more than 20 feet away, don't risk it. Just drop to the ground.

According to police, most bullets are fired between 3 and 6 feet above the ground. So the chances of being hit if you are lying flat are small. Lie perfectly still. Don't move around or try to crawl to a better spot if the gunshots are continuing. Don't draw any attention to yourself.

If the gunfire stops, don't jump up immediately. The shooter may just be reloading. Stay where you are for at least a minute or more after the gunfire has stopped. Because you still can't be absolutely sure that the shooting has stopped, once you get up, get into a building quickly. Don't go back out until you know it's over.

are hungry or thirsty, accepting things from strangers can be a dangerous practice. Most strangers will mean no harm, it's true. Even so, stay on the safe side, and politely say "No, thank you." Most important of all, never accept an alcoholic beverage or drugs of any kind from anyone.

Older kids sometimes think it's funny to see younger kids get high. Some even like to get kids "hooked" so they will become customers and start buying drugs. You must be very strong about this. If you are in a public place and know that alcoholic beverages, marijuana, crack, or other drugs are being used, stay away from those using them. And if one of your friends insists on trying it, *don't you!* Concentrate on enjoying the game or the concert. If anything that is going on around you makes you feel uneasy, or threatened, gather up your things, and your friends, and find an usher or security guard. Perhaps you can be seated somewhere else. If not, you can always leave. Your parents or guardians will be glad to pick you up early rather than have you stay in a place where you don't feel safe.

If you are in a place where a fight breaks out, get away from the action quickly. Don't stay to watch. It's easy to get injured should the fight spread and spill into the area where you're watching. And that can happen very quickly.

Also watch out for lone adults in public places. If you see an adult hanging out in a place where kids gather, stay away from him. Perhaps he's someone's parent. If not, he may well be up to no good. And if an adult approaches you offering to pay for an arcade game, food, a magazine or anything else, refuse quickly. Use the same rules that apply on the street. Don't be friendly and smiling. Be cold and very firm. Then move away quickly. If he follows you, look for someone in authority.

You and your friends can have a good time when you start going out on your own. But you still must be careful all the time. Stay alert to what's going on around you. In many cases, being aware can help you to avoid dangerous situations.

5

STAYING SAFE
AT SCHOOL

Today, the bad things that happen in schools probably get more media attention than the good. It seems that schools have become danger zones in many ways for children from elementary to high school. And the incidents that end up in the newspapers, or on the TV news, are not confined to so-called inner-city schools. There are violent incidents that include beatings, stabbings, shootings, students held hostage by either another student or a deranged adult. Teachers are often at just as much risk as the students.

While these are extreme cases that don't happen too often, the everyday world of the modern student is not always a safe and carefree one. According to Ed Muir, of New York City's United Federation of Teachers, petty theft is the single biggest problem kids face in school. But there are also problems of cliques, gangs, and bullies. Sometimes these groups and individuals try to extort money from other children using the threat of physical violence.

Because of these threats, many students carry weapons into the schools, including guns and knives. Other students, fearing violence, pretend to be sick so they can stay home, or they simply skip school without letting their parents or guardians know.

Threats to their safety put kids at risk traveling to and from school, in the schoolyard, the lunchroom, the hallways and the rest rooms. Some children become victims and learn the hard way that they need to protect themselves. Others learn from friends or older brothers and sisters who have had problems and can give good advice about dangers to avoid.

According to experts, a problem such as petty theft usually begins at about the seventh-grade level. That doesn't mean isolated cases can't happen sooner. In fact, there is evidence that these kinds of things are now happening with younger and younger children.

There are many theories as to why schools have become breeding grounds for small crime, gang activity, and violence. Some experts feel it's just an extension of things that are happening on the streets. Others feel that students, especially those in badly overcrowded schools, begin to feel alone and alienated. The hallways, dining hall, and schoolyard all become almost mob scenes.

In these schools, many students don't form close relationships with others or with teachers. While some students join cliques and gangs, alienated students are alone and are often the victims of others. Large schools with shrinking budgets have fewer activities for the students. The kids, in turn, have more free time. Some kids are in and out of school several times during the day. It's not always a healthy climate.

HOW HIGH IS THE RISK?

Studies by the National Institute of Education (NIE) have revealed some interesting facts about problems in schools. Most incidents of theft and personal violence, as well as disruptions of the rules, occur during school hours and most often in the middle of the week. There are also more minor incidents at the junior high level than in the high schools.

The NIE also found that the highest risk of incident occurred in the hallways and stairwells between classes. There are also safety risks in lunchrooms, locker rooms, rest rooms, and gymnasiums. Chances of being a victim of an assault or

The dramatic increase in weapons in schools has forced some communities to install metal detectors at school entrances. Students are checked for weapons as they enter the building for the day.

robbery decrease as students move to the higher grades. Seventh graders are the most likely to be attacked or robbed, while high school seniors (twelfth graders) are the safest.

The majority of school violence involves students of the same race. However, there is more chance of minority students being victims if the school has 70 percent or better of majority students. It doesn't matter if that majority is white, black, or hispanic. In addition, the NIE found that school and class size are also important factors when considering school safety.

In schools where teachers and administrators establish personal relationships with students, there is less chance of crime and violence. The risk of so-called minor attacks is the same everywhere. But the more serious, more violent attacks usually occur in big-city schools.

WHAT CAN YOU DO TO STAY SAFE?

Many schools today have groups and organizations to promote school spirit and awareness. One of their goals is to keep crime and violence to a minimum. These groups are often made up of students, teachers, administrators, and sometimes even parents or guardians. They discuss problems that have occurred and try to work out ways to keep them from happening again, or from getting worse. They also put students together to talk about potential problems and to try to ease tensions at the school.

If there is a group like this at your school, you might think about becoming involved. If there is no room to join, then try to learn who the members are. If you have something to say, then contact a member. Most groups try to involve, and get input from, as many students as possible.

It is also important for you as an individual to become known. Make as many friends as possible from the various groups at your school. The more people who know you as an individual—that is, know your name—the less chance you have of becoming a victim. There are several reasons for this.

*Joining clubs at school can
help you to make friends and have fun.
You'll also keep yourself from
being the kind of anonymous student
who makes an easy target.*

For one thing, people looking for targets tend to pick alienated loners they don't know and who don't really know them. The black kid, the white kid, the fat kid, the tall kid, are all potential victims. But Leroy, Janice, Freddy, or Tom have names and identities. They are less likely to be targets. And if you know the names of a great many kids, you are more likely to be able to identify anyone who bothers you. That, too, is a way to protect yourself.

By now you will not be surprised to hear that you should try to avoid being isolated at school. Go to and from school in groups. It's also best to stay where the crowds are—in the schoolyards, hallways, lunchrooms and even rest rooms. Try to use the rest rooms between classes, when a lot of kids are there. If you're slow changing in the locker room, ask one or two friends to wait for you. Safety in numbers is something that really works, no matter where you are.

You should also try to become involved in some extracurricular activities—sports, clubs, cheerleading, student council, or band. You can make more friends that way, which is important, and help foster school spirit. And more people will know who *you* are.

And something else is important. Be careful not to wear clothing that draws attention to you, or that makes you stand out in a crowd. Perhaps doing this robs you of some individuality. But remember, you want to stay safe. Blending in is one way to do it.

DEALING WITH GANGS AND BULLIES

There have always been cliques and gangs in schools, made up of both boys and girls. Sometimes they are linked by a group name. Sometimes they wear jackets. An organized group doesn't necessarily mean danger. But there are gangs in some schools who prey on others. Once a gang starts illegal or violent activity, school officials need to take immediate action.

PEER MEDIATION

Many schools train students to act as mediators to calm conflicts between other students. With fellow students handling mediation, the disputants know they will not be punished or put down. Kids like to be heard and not judged, and for these reasons peer mediation has been successful at many middle and high schools throughout the United States.

Peer mediation is not something that is taken lightly. Participating schools view it as a long-term situation in which the mediators are carefully chosen and trained. At a midsize New York State junior-senior high school, peer mediation has now been in effect for five years. Here's how it works:

The original group of mediators was trained by Project Team, a federally funded organization formed to combat substance abuse. The school keeps a group of twelve to fifteen trained student mediators, grades seven to twelve. As the older mediators graduate, new ones are trained. There are mediators at each grade level, and most stick with it through their secondary school years.

Mediators have thirty to forty hours of training, learning skills they will have for a lifetime. These include various questioning techniques, communication skills, the art of confidentiality, and how to recognize danger signals that require a referral. In other words, knowing when to bring someone else into a situation.

There is always an adult present during mediations, but not always in the same room. The adult might be on the other side of a glass door or, if the room is large, across the room out of hearing range. There are always two mediators to question two disputants. Mediators do not handle any situation that involves weapons, drugs, or alcohol.

Mediators can take notes during the sessions, but will tear up the notes in front of the disputants before they leave. This helps to ensure confidentiality. Mediators are not there to punish or take sides. Their objective is to allow the two disputants to reach their own solution to their problems. Once the disputants reach a solution, it is written down and signed by the disputants. If it doesn't work, they can go back to mediation a second time.

In most cases, there is an opening statement by the mediators. After that, the two disputants talk to the mediators, one at a time. Sometimes they speak to each other, but mostly to the mediators. Once the mediators have heard each side, they repeat what they have heard, then begin asking questions. The questions are designed to bring out the true feelings of the disputants.

Finally, the mediators will ask the disputants what *they* would like to see happen. The aim then is to reach a solution both disputants can accept.

Most mediations involve relationships and "he said–she said" situations. Fights are also referred to mediators. The disputants have a choice of accepting mediation and being suspended one day, or rejecting mediation and being suspended five days. Group mediations are rare. Only the strongest mediators are allowed to deal with cliques, gangs, and clubs that have problems with each other.

At the New York school that is being used as an example here, peer mediation has been very successful. It has gotten students involved and given them a way to help build morale within their school. It has also cut down significantly on the need for discipline by teachers and administrators.

Though mediation does not put an end to problems at a school, it can help students to understand those problems and understand themselves better at the same time.

One of the most common of the illegal gang activities in schools involves gang members extorting money from their schoolmates. They usually do this under threat of physical harm. Some kids are so frightened they don't even tell their parents. They lie and say they need money for some kind of school activity. The money then goes to the gang, because the victim wants to avoid a beating.

What should you do if you are threatened in school? This is often a tough call and very difficult for kids to handle. If several older kids are threatening you, telling you if you don't pay you will be hurt, it's a frightening thing. Gangs also will tell a victim that if he tells his parents or school officials, they will get him for it. They tell the victim that no matter what he does, he cannot escape. They'll be watching.

There is no doubt that this can be a very frightening experience for any kid. If this happens to you, you may feel alone and helpless. But if you do not tell your parents, guardians, or school officials, you will continue to be a victim. Waiting almost always makes things worse.

It isn't an easy thing if a gang singles you out and wants money. Sometimes they may demand your lunch or your bus pass. If you feel you are in personal danger and cornered by the gang, give them what they want. But remember, even once you do this, their demands may not stop. You must talk to your parents, guardians, or school officials immediately. Tell them what happened. If you tell your parents or guardians first, make sure they contact your school right away. Some schools have networks set up to handle this very kind of thing. Together, your parents, guardians, or school officials will decide if the police should be called in to handle the situation. Let the adults decide the best way to handle your problem while protecting you at the same time.

Bullies are yet another problem often faced in a school setting. This is usually a situation where a bigger or older kid picks on a younger or smaller one. This is not necessarily a situation where the object is to gain money or possessions. It's more a matter of power and intimidation. And it can be quite frightening.

There are many psychological reasons why someone becomes a bully. He may be someone who is having problems at home. He may be a victim of abuse by an older brother or parent. Or he himself may have been the victim of a bully at one time or another. There is no set rule to dealing with this kind of person.

Sometimes you can talk to a bully and make him realize that what he is doing is wrong, that he has nothing to gain by picking on you. Another alternative is to fight. Bullies often like to intimidate, but often they are really not ready to get into a bad fight. But there is no way of knowing this ahead of time.

As a rule, fighting should be a last resort. If the bully is much bigger and stronger than you, it might be silly to fight. If he begins to push you around, running for help is not a bad idea. Because you don't want to risk a bad beating, there is nothing wrong with getting away. That doesn't make you a coward or a wimp—just as telling a parent or school official doesn't make you a squealer or tattletale. You have a right to feel safe at your school. Don't let a bully take that away from you.

In dealing with a bully, you must try to size up the situation. You don't want to risk a beating, yet you can't let the bully continue to intimidate you. You've got to find the best way to put a stop to it. Talking to an adult should be step number one.

A FEW OTHER TIPS

Here are a few other tips for staying safe in school and keeping yourself from being ripped off:

1. Never put your wallet, watch, or any other valuables out in the open while changing in the locker room. All it takes is for you to look away for a split second and they may be gone.

2. Don't leave any kind of valuables in a desk or even in a locker if it isn't very secure. Never give the combination of your locker to anyone else, unless the person is a friend you know you can trust. (And don't write your combination down anywhere where someone else can find it. Losing a notebook or a wallet is bad enough, but things can get even worse if someone finds your combination and uses it to clean out your locker.)

3. Don't leave your purse unattended in the rest room. In fact, it isn't a good idea to take off your rings while washing up. Remember, petty theft is the biggest single crime in schools in the United States.

4. Keep valuable possessions like an expensive walkman, a baseball card collection, or special items of jewelry at home. If you bring them to school, you risk losing them.

5. Stay away from crowds in the schoolyard or in the hallways if your instincts tell you something bad is happening, like a fight or mugging. Get help instead.

6. Never accept an offer of "free" drugs of any kind from anyone in and around your school. This cannot be emphasized enough. In fact, don't take anything to eat or drink from another person unless it's someone you know very well.

7. Don't enter a rest room or any other room if there seems to be a student "standing guard" at the door. Something may be happening inside that you don't want to get involved with.

8. Don't allow your friends to convince you to do something your instincts tells you is wrong. This kind of pressure is called peer pressure, and it can be very hard to stand up to. Don't take dares or break school rules just to impress another person or group.

9. Finally, take pride in yourself and your school. You are there to get an education that will help you later in life. Don't let others take that opportunity away from you.

6

DANGER FROM STRANGERS

One of the biggest fears for parents today is the fear of a stranger luring their child off the street and taking her away forever. It's unfortunate that parents should have to worry about this kind of thing, but their fears are real. Studies have shown that children fear the danger posed by strangers, as well.

In fact, being kidnapped is one of the things that children worry most about in today's world. Kids see reports about kidnappings on the television or in newspapers. They worry about whether or not such a thing might happen to them. Although it's a shame that kids have to worry about these things, it's good that they do. Because the more they are aware of what might happen, the more they will avoid going off with a total stranger.

Stranger-danger is a very real threat. Adults who want to abduct children or harm them in some way usually have a number of ways to persuade a kid to go with them. It can be done on foot, on a motorbike, or in a car. Unsuspecting children will often go along, thinking this nice person is going to help them, give them a lift, allow them to have some fun, or take them where they need to go.

Children need to be taught not to be fooled by these tricks. It's up to parents, guardians, and other adults to warn their kids about some of the lures strangers will use. It's worth rehearsing some of these potential situations at home so you will be ready, and know what to do, if you are confronted on the street.

WHOM CAN YOU TRUST?

What makes stranger-danger so difficult for children to deal with is that there is no way to tell a bad stranger from a good stranger just by looking at him. From the time they were able to walk and talk, most kids have met many strangers who were nice and kind. They usually met these strangers through their parents and relatives.

Ever since you were a young child, you've grown accustomed to strangers saying such things as "What a big boy you're getting to be." Or "What a pretty dress you're wearing." And you have been taught to politely answer such questions as "How old are you?" or "What grade are you in at school?"

But there comes a time when you can't be friendly to strangers anymore. Once again, this is often a matter of learning not to be nice. When you were very young, you were always with your parents or a relative when you met strangers. It was all right to be polite and nice then. But now that you are on your own, even when you're with friends, the time has come to put your guard up, especially when you're alone on the street.

A stranger may truly be nice. But you don't know that. The stranger may also have bad intentions. You don't know that, either. Now is the time to be careful, not nice. Now it's time to be safe.

DEALING WITH STRANGERS

A stranger is anyone you don't know. It may be a police officer, a shopkeeper, or a school crossing guard. If you don't know him, he's a stranger. Strangers like these are usually friendly and helpful people. They might say hi to you as you cross the street or go into their stores. It's certainly all right to say hi back. Even if a stranger on a street says hi, you might give a quick reply. There's no harm in that.

Most strangers are nice people. Many of them, like police officers and school crossing guards, are watching out for you. Other strangers will help if they see you in trouble. Many have children of their own. The problem is that there is no completely safe way to tell a good stranger from a bad stranger.

So if a stranger stops and begins asking you questions like "What's your name?" or "Where do you live?" it's time to end the conversation. Don't answer, just keep walking quickly and confidently. If the stranger begins walking after you, then run to the nearest building or toward a group of people.

Don't ever answer any personal questions from a stranger.

In fact, don't answer no matter how nice that stranger seems. A smiling, kindly-looking stranger can sometimes be more of a threat than a tough-talking, gruff one. And that's the point. You don't know.

TRICKS TO PREPARE FOR

There are a number of tricks that strangers with bad intentions will use if they want children to go with them. For starters, there is one rule that all kids should obey without exception:

Never take a walk or go for a ride with a stranger!

If you follow this rule faithfully, you will definitely reduce your risk of danger coming from a stranger. But there are also many ways strangers try to make it seem that you *should* go with them. Most of these tricks involve promises, a need for help, or an outright lie. Let's take a look at some of the most common ways strangers get kids to go with them:

1. **"Do you want something to eat?"** This is one of the oldest and simplest tricks. A stranger will ask a kid if he's hungry and offer him food. He might say, "I'm heading to McDonald's. Wanna go?" Or "I have some great candy back at my place."

   If someone tries to tempt you with food, give them a curt "No, thanks," or "Not hungry," and walk away quickly.

2. "There's a great movie playing nearby. Wanna go?" Asking a child to go to an attractive event is another common trick. It could be a movie. It could be an amusement park, an arcade, a circus, a magic show—anything that most kids want to see.

   Don't be tempted, even if it's something you want to see very badly. Say no and walk away. Remember rule number one and never go anywhere with a stranger.

3. "I've lost my poor little puppy. Would you help me look for him?" This is an old trick and often a successful one because most kids love puppies and feel bad if a puppy is lost. Even if the story is true, you cannot take the chance and be nice. Not even if a little old lady is the one asking for help. Be safe. Say you're meeting someone and running late. Then walk away.

4. "Could you help me carry these packages? I have a broken arm and it hurts." Sure enough, the stranger is juggling several packages and one arm is in a sling. But your answer should still be no. Walk away. Some people have been known to fake a broken arm just to get a kid to help them. You don't know what the truth is and cannot take a chance. Keep your guard up.

5. "I'm new in the neighborhood and really lost. Could you help me find Recreation Park?" That's easy, you think. You know how to get to Recreation Park. Your reaction may be to carefully explain or even to go along to show the way. Don't. You shouldn't go anywhere with a stranger. And if the stranger is sitting in a car, be especially cautious. Don't get close enough so that he can suddenly leap out and pull you in. Just say you don't know and keep walking.

6. "Hey, isn't this a great motorbike I got? Wanna go for a ride?" A lot of kids love dirt bikes and motorcycles. If a stranger pulls up on a sharp new bike and asks you to hop on, it might be tough to resist. But is it worth the risk? Remember rule number one. Say no and walk away.

7. "Your mother has been hurt in an accident. I was sent to bring you to her at the hospital." This is one of the cruelest ways to trick

a child into getting into a vehicle. Any kid would react to such horrible news with fear for his mother. And an upset and panicky kid will often jump into a car without thinking. If you should find yourself in a situation like that, you will have to fight off the strong urge to go with the person. Again you must say no. Never believe a stranger who tells you about a family emergency. If there is a real emergency, someone you know will come to get you.

There is one trick you and your parents can use to protect you from strangers. Decide on a secret password. If your parents send a stranger to pick you up, that stranger should say the password immediately. Otherwise, don't go with him or her.

8. **"I'm a police officer. There's been some vandalism and my captain wants you at the station for questioning. Here's my badge."** If the stranger is not in a police uniform and not driving what you can recognize as a real police car, don't go. Anyone can get a fake badge that looks real at a quick glance. Maybe someone you know can help you verify that the person really is a police officer. If you have any doubts at all, don't go.

9. **"Hi, Maria. Remember me? I'm a friend of your father's."** Don't be tricked into trusting a stranger just because they know your name. Think about it. Is your name on your jacket or backpack? Did your friends just say good-bye to you and the stranger overhear them? The stranger may act hurt that you don't remember him, or tell you that you're being rude. Never mind. It's better to be safe than foolishly polite.

These are just some of the basic tricks used by strangers looking to harm or abduct children. There is no need to run immediately. Just walk away quickly and confidently. If the stranger begins to follow you, then use the rules you learned in Chapter Three. Run to the nearest building or person in authority. Or get into a crowd of people quickly.

And *never* hitchhike. You just don't know who will pick you up!

*The rules concerning
hitchhiking are easy to
remember: don't do it.*

Stranger-danger is something every young person must know how to handle and avoid. Talk about it at home and in school. You and your parents and friends can even act out some of the situations described in this section. That way, if a stranger approaches you, you'll know exactly what to do.

WHAT ABOUT SELF-DEFENSE?

The subject of self-defense in any of these dangerous situations has always been open to debate. No one would ask a 75-pound child to take on a 175-pound attacker. And no one expects that you will suddenly become the Karate Kid. Many kids who find themselves thrust into potentially violent situations have never been there before.

So, what to do? If you are in a dangerous situation, do you fight? There are some experts who feel the best defense is to be aware of your surroundings and be ready to escape. In other cases, just saying no can save your life.

There was a case in Portland, Oregon, when a man asked two young children to help him find his lost puppy in the nearby woods. They said no and kept walking. A short time later another child was murdered in the area and the killer caught shortly afterward. The two kids saw his picture in the paper and told their mother he was the man who asked them to find his lost puppy.

Here's another kind of self-defense. In 1994, a twelve-year-old girl from Pittsfield, Massachusetts, was walking to school when a strange man began walking beside her. He suddenly showed her a gun. He told her to do everything he said and she would be OK.

The girl had been part of a D.A.R.E. (Drug Abuse Resistance Education Project) program since kindergarten. When the man told her to get into a nearby pickup truck, she knew she had to act fast.

"I knew if I got in, I'd end up in a ditch someplace," the girl said later. So instead she suddenly began breathing very heavily. She told the man she was hyperventilating and had to sit down to catch her breath. She started to take off her backpack as she continued to breathe very hard.

Then, suddenly, she made a break for it. The man lunged for her but could only grab the backpack as she slipped it off. She then ran as fast as she could and got away. Later, the same man was caught and linked to a number of child kidnappings and murders. The girl said that being part of D.A.R.E. had saved her life.

THE POWER YELL

Another nonphysical method of self-defense is called the *power yell*. This is not a regular scream. It is described as a yell that comes from deep in the stomach. It's like a yell that a martial arts expert uses before an attack. So it isn't a mark of fright. Rather, it's a sign of attack.

The power yell can serve a dual purpose. It can help you overcome your fear in a critical situation. It serves to break the ice when you feel panic setting in and think you might freeze. At the same time, it can startle an attacker, perhaps just enough for you to have a chance to escape.

You should use the power yell very quickly in an attack. The sooner the better. If you yell *before* the attacker puts his hands on you, there is a better chance it will frighten him off or give you the chance to escape. Most potential molesters or abductors aren't expecting a big, loud, aggressive yell from a small person. However, if the attacker has already grabbed you, the yell might make him angry or more violent.

No form of self-defense is foolproof. And whether or not to defend yourself is always a judgment call only you can make. There is no way anyone can guarantee that self-defense will work. That's why it's important to get advice from the experts. Join groups such as D.A.R.E., and talk to people who have experience in safety and crime prevention.

PHYSICAL SELF-DEFENSE

No one can tell you that you have to fight in certain situations. There is no set rule for who fights and who doesn't, or when. The use of physical force to thwart danger must be up to the individual. For many years, police officials had advised both women and young children not to physically resist an attack.

But in recent years, with many people taking classes in martial arts or carrying weapons of some kind, people have tended to fight back more often. This is not necessarily a good thing. There are times when it works, and times when it doesn't. That's why an individual must assess the situation before deciding what to do. There are several things that must be considered:

1. **Is the attacker carrying a weapon?** If the attacker has a gun, physical resistance is certainly unwise. If he has a knife, resistance is still risky, especially without special training. A club or other such weapon swings the odds somewhat in favor of resistance, but there is still risk of serious injury or worse.

   Statistics show that only about one-third of attackers use weapons, and the percentage drops even more among those who attack children and teens.

2. **What is the overall danger level you are facing?** If you are attacked in an area where there are people nearby, yelling and physical resistance could buy you time until help arrives. Likewise, if there is safety a short distance away, you will be better off trying to break loose and run. If you are in a completely isolated area, the danger level is clearly greater.

3. **Do you have confidence in your ability to fight?** Physical force will undoubtedly be met with physical force. A halfhearted effort to resist won't work. You must be willing to generate real anger and fight very hard. If you don't feel capable of doing this, then don't.

4. **What kind of physical training have you had?** The more training you have had in the martial arts or other forms of self-defense,

*Martial arts training can increase
your self-confidence tremendously.
Just be sure it doesn't lead you
to take foolish risks.*

the better your chances of resisting successfully will be. If you've had no training and have never been involved in physical confrontation, your chances probably aren't very good.

These are all points that must be considered and evaluated very quickly if you are attacked or if someone is attempting to abduct you. If it's a situation where you feel your life may be at stake (someone trying to drag you into a vehicle, for example), you are probably better off yelling, screaming, kicking, and trying everything to attract attention and/or escape.

If you decide to study self-defense, you should do it right. Find out where classes are held in the method you want to learn. Then practice very hard. You can't learn to defend yourself from reading about techniques in a book. Just as you can't learn how to hit a baseball from reading a book. You can read about the fundamentals, but you learn by doing it.

There are certainly success stories of children under the age of ten who have escaped adult attackers by surprising them with learned self-defense skills. It can be done. But it's not something that should be taken lightly.

Strangers do pose potential dangers. There is no getting away from that in today's world. The more you know about dealing with this stranger-danger, the better you will feel about yourself. The more confident you are, the more likely you will be to remain safe.

PARENTAL ABDUCTION

There are times when a child is abducted by one of his own parents. That's right. Parents sometimes kidnap their own children. This usually happens when the parents are getting or have already gotten a divorce. There is always a question of which parent will get the child or children and how often the other parent will get to see them.

Some parents, however, are so upset and angry about the

divorce that they can't make the right decision about the future of the children. Sometimes a parent who loses custody in a court of law decides to just take the children and then hide from the other parent. This is against the law.

There are other reasons, too, why a parent may want to take the children and run. This is not always in the best interest of the kids. If you are taken away by a parent against the ruling of a court or against your wishes, you may live a very different kind of life. And it may not be a happy one.

There are a few things a young person can do to learn if a parent is trying to run off with him:

1. Never leave town with either your father or your mother without saying good-bye to the other parent. Ask to call or see the other parent in person.
2. If one parent begins packing your things and says you are going on a trip and must leave right away, try to contact your other parent to see if it's OK.
3. If your parents are divorced and you are visiting the parent who doesn't have custody, always check with the other parent before going on a trip to another city. Find out if the other parent knows about it.

Sometimes a parent taking you away will not let you make a call. And sometimes a parent will have the children kidnapped by professionals and brought to them. If you are taken like that, there are also some things you can do:

1. Always memorize the phone number and address of the parent you live with.
2. Know how to make a collect call or a 911 call. Find out how to do this from a phone booth as well as a house phone.
3. Know the phone numbers of a close relative or other adult you trust.
4. If you are kidnapped by a parent and get away, go to a police officer or call the police from a phone immediately. Follow all the

other rules in this chapter about strangers. Always seek someone in authority. You are safer going into a store for help than asking a stranger on the street.

Because kids usually trust their parents, you may not realize right away that you are really being kidnapped. But when a parent won't tell you where you are going or won't let you say good-bye to anyone, especially the parent who is being left behind, think hard about what's happening.

Angry parents who take their children will often tell lies about the other parent. "Mommy is dead!" Or "Daddy doesn't want you anymore." Children can sometimes be fooled by this. But you should insist on hearing it from someone else, another adult you trust.

If you are in a situation where you are taken by a parent and kept away from the other parent, it is *never* your fault. It is the fault of the parent who has taken you. And that parent is breaking the law.

DEALING WITH SEXUAL ABUSE

One of the biggest dangers for young people on the streets is that someone older will try to sexually abuse them. Sexual abuse can be anything from someone passing sexual remarks to you, rubbing up against you, grabbing you in what should be private areas of your body, exposing themselves to you, or trying to perform sexual acts with you.

Sexual assault or attempted sexual assault can happen to boys as well as girls. No one should be forced to do anything against their will or have anything done to them that they don't want. A person's first dignity is his right over his own body. Don't let anyone try to convince you that you don't have that right. You do.

People who try to sexually abuse or assault kids are sick. They do not look upon their victims as human beings with feelings. Both the victim's feelings and personality are being ignored. Yet victims can come away from this terrible experience with feelings of guilt. They feel degraded and worthless. It is as if all their dignity has been stripped away. These feelings are often difficult to overcome. Sometimes they can linger for years. In many cases, getting professional help in dealing with incidents of sexual abuse is a very good idea.

TAKING STEPS TO PROTECT YOURSELF

Sexual offenders will often pick on young people because they see an easy target. They don't expect any resistance. In other

*Although you may want to
answer when someone
verbally abuses you, the best
response is to walk away.*

words, they figure young people will basically stand there and let it happen. That's because innocent children who have not been warned about these things and are not aware of them often *will* just stand there.

It doesn't have to be that way. You are going to be spending a lot of time on the street and in public places. If you sense that someone is about to try or is trying something sexual, there are things you can do.

Many girls and women will encounter verbal abuse from boys or men, often in groups. These men will stare, whistle, and shout things about your body and what they might like to do to you. This is not flattery. It's an act of hostility and a rather immature one at that.

Don't dignify these people with an answer. If you see a group harassing other girls in this way, don't walk past them. Cross the street instead. If you find yourself the object of lewd remarks, pretend you don't even hear them. Just keep walking. If anyone begins to follow you, you know what to do. Look for a police officer or other authority figure, or go into a building or shop and call for help.

Another common sexual act against young people is called *flashing*. This is when a man exposes his genitals and/or begins masturbating in public. People have been known to do this on buses or trains, on street corners, or in playgrounds and parks where groups of young people gather.

Experts feel these flashers get their pleasure from the looks of horror and disgust on the faces of their victims. These kinds of exhibitionists can be adults of all ages, as well as young boys. The safest way to deal with a flasher is to pretend not to see what he is doing. Then get away as quickly as you can.

If you see that same person hanging around your school or playground, tell your parents, guardians, or a teacher. It's also a good idea to report him to the police. Flashers are often not difficult to catch and what they are doing is against the law.

If you must travel on crowded
public transportation, keep your
guard up. If you think ahead about
what sort of problems you
might encounter, it can sometimes
help you to avoid trouble.

Some people will take advantage of a crowded street, hall-way, bus, or train. They will stand real close and begin rubbing up against you, or touching you with their hands so that others in the crowd cannot see. The same basic rules apply that were mentioned in Chapter Four about being bothered in crowds.

If you can move away, do so. Then tell someone in author-ity. If you can't move away because of the crowd, don't just stand there and take it. Yell out that someone is bothering you. Make a fuss about it. Since most molesters expect young victims to freeze, calling attention to what is going on will usually get them to stop and even move away.

OTHER KINDS OF MOLESTERS

One type of molester who preys on children is called a pe-dophile. Before they molest a child, they will often make an ef-fort to befriend him. They look for solitary youngsters who appear lonely, friendless, and neglected. At first, they act like a big brother. They might take the child to different places, buy him presents, and take a real interest in his life and talk to him sincerely about his problems.

A pedophile will try to make his victim totally dependent on him. Only then, will he begin to make sexual advances. This type of molestation is often started on the streets or in public places, though the pedophile may have a house or apartment where he will eventually take his victim. The pedophile doesn't have to be a stranger. He may also be a relative or acquaintance.

If the child resists at this point, the pedophile will again try to talk his victim into cooperating. He will threaten to tell the victim's mother. He will tell the child that they both can get into real trouble, that he might go to jail. Then he'll remind the child what a good friend he's been. He may also dare the child to tell someone, insisting that no one will believe a child who ac-cuses a respected adult.

Pedophiles are usually young to middle-aged men, though

occasionally they may be women, or older men, as well. Outwardly most appear very normal. So once again you must be wary. If someone singles you out and seems overly nice, don't take a chance. Don't let that person buy you presents and don't go anywhere with him, not even to a public place where you feel safe.

And remember, if someone comes up and introduces himself to you, don't give out your name, your address, or any other personal information. And don't introduce that person to any of your friends. It isn't worth the risk.

Some potential molesters will get themselves into positions where they work with young children. They might be scout leaders, teachers, coaches, big brothers, camp counselors, or youth organization workers. The majority of these people are not molesters. But a few are.

If you feel that any adult working with you touches you in a way that makes you feel uncomfortable, or suggests you do something that makes you uncomfortable, get away from him immediately. Then tell your parents, guardians, or someone in authority what has happened.

There is one important thing, however, that you should realize. A charge of molesting children is a very serious one. A person charged with child molestation may lose his job and his family and may even go to jail. Don't ever make up a story about someone molesting you. There have been cases where children have done this because they were angry at an adult for some other reason. This is *not* the way to show your anger. You may ruin an innocent person's life in the process.

8

HOME ALONE

According to the National Child Care Survey (NCCS), there are an estimated 2.5 million latchkey kids living in the United States today. This number includes not only kids in big cities, but those in suburbs across the country as well. It is also estimated that some 6 million kids spend part of every day alone.

A latchkey kid is a young person who comes home from school to an empty house or apartment. The numbers have grown steadily in the last few decades for several reasons. The two-income household has increased steadily. More and more women have entered the workforce, and in many families both parents work full-time jobs. There are also many more single-parent households where that parent—whether it be a mother or a father—is working full-time.

Experts differ on the age at which children can safely become latchkey kids. Many feel the earliest age is ten. Some feel it should be twelve, but still others say that children should be at least fourteen before they can be fully trusted to stay safe and handle various situations that might arise.

In a sense, it depends on the intelligence and maturity of the child. Your parents or guardians will be the ones to decide if you are ready to be on your own. Here are just some qualities and characteristics that will indicate whether or not you are ready to become a latchkey kid:

1. You must be able to amuse yourself when left alone.
2. You must be able to handle household chores and responsibilities on your own.
3. You must be able to talk maturely with adults other than your parents or guardians—relatives, neighbors, or the parents of your friends.
4. You must be able to think for yourself and solve minor problems in a sensible way.
5. You must be able to talk to your parents about any fears you have or any problems that arise.
6. You must be able to act decisively in situations that require a quick decision.
7. You must *want* to try being a latchkey kid.

These are just some of the things families must discuss before deciding that a child will be able to come home from school and let themselves into an empty house with their own key. Once you become a latchkey kid, you'll have a big responsibility every day. And you'll also have to watch out for potential danger so that you can protect yourself. After all, there will be no one else home to do it for you.

CARRYING THE KEY

One of the first responsibilities a latchkey kid has is carrying and protecting the house key. For starters, don't ever put a name or address on the key or keychain. That way, someone finding a lost key won't know whose it is.

If your door has more than one lock, color-code the keys to the locks so you know which fits which. That eliminates fumbling and guesswork. Practice letting yourself in. This will give you confidence that you can use your keys quickly and correctly.

If, for some reason, your key doesn't work one day, go to a neighbor and ask for help. Don't try to force the key. Someone may have jammed the lock.

You can carry your key on a chain around your neck or on a chain attached to a belt loop with the key tucked into your pocket. Always keep the key out of sight. You don't want to let the wrong people know you are a latchkey kid. Knowing you will be home alone, someone might follow you. And don't tell anyone, even a friend, about the key. That friend may tell someone else, who may tell someone else. Sooner or later, the wrong person may find out that you're home alone every day.

Always make sure your parents or guardians have left a spare key with a neighbor or relative you can contact if you lose your key. Don't leave the spare key under a mat or in the mailbox. Those are places where burglars always look.

DANGERS TO WATCH FOR

While you are alone at home, there are a number of home-related dangers you might face. These are discussed in *Hazards at Home*, another book in this series, and won't be repeated here. However, there are some other dangers latchkey kids face related to coming and going, and dealing with strangers.

If you live in an apartment building, you might have to take an elevator to reach your floor. Muggers have been known to use elevators to trap people. There are several important precautions to take when riding an elevator on a daily basis:

1. Never get on an elevator with someone who makes you nervous. If the elevator stops and there is someone like that in the car, pretend you have forgotten something. Tell him to go ahead. Then you can take the stairs, or wait for the elevator to return.
2. If you get on an empty elevator, check the control panel to see where the elevator is going. If you see it's heading for the basement, hit the "door open" button quickly and get off. Muggers sometimes wait in basements and try to bring the elevator down to them with a potential victim inside.
3. Always stand alongside the control panel and watch the door. Look directly at people who enter the elevator. This gives you a

confident look and alerts you right away when someone you might not trust gets on. If you just daydream or stand looking at the floor, you lose any small advantage you might have. You might also lose the chance to get off the elevator quickly.

4. If someone gets on after you and makes you nervous, push the button for the nearest floor and get off. If you are followed off the elevator, begin calling for help. (Remember, people are more likely to open their doors if you yell "Fire" than if you simply yell for help.) Try to go to an area where there are people.

5. If your building does not have a doorman or if there have been problems in the elevators in the past, you might consider always using the stairs. If someone appears on a stairway, at least there is a chance to escape. Inside an elevator, you're simply trapped.

Always be aware of your surroundings as you approach your door and put the key in the lock. There are crimes known as "push-in" crimes where the perpetrator waits in hiding. As soon as someone opens their door, he comes up behind them and pushes them inside, trapping them in their own house or apartment.

If anyone is lurking close to your doorway, or if you sense someone is nearby, don't approach your door. If you are in an apartment building, keep walking. Either run down the stairs to find help or go to a neighbor's door and knock. (But be careful there, too. Someone could push in when your neighbor opens the door.)

If you live in a house, make sure you haven't been followed home and no strangers are watching you. If there are big, thick bushes near your door, ask your parents or guardians either to remove them or to trim them back so no one can hide there waiting for you to come home and unlock the door.

Should you sense someone is following you or perhaps hiding near your door, don't go in. Go to a neighbor's house instead, tell them what happened, and have them call the police.

Always check the house when you come home from school.

If something doesn't look right to you, don't go in. It may be a light burning that wasn't on when you left. Perhaps a window is open that you know was closed. Or maybe you hear some sound coming from inside the house, as if someone is moving about. Don't take a chance. Go to a neighbor immediately and call the police.

WHEN YOU'RE HOME ALONE

You are going to have a great many responsibilities when you're home alone. You've got to keep busy, watch the house, maybe keep an eye on a younger brother or sister, take care of a pet, and follow all the rules your parents or guardians have made for you. But you will still have to make some decisions about things happening unexpectedly, or things that you can't control.

Strangers will sometimes call on the telephone. Never tell a stranger that you are home alone. Instead, tell callers who ask for your parents or guardians that they can't come to the phone right now but you'll take the number and they will return the call soon.

You should also never reveal your name or phone number to someone you don't know. If you answer the phone and someone immediately asks you, "Who's this?" don't tell them. Instead, ask whom they want to speak with. If they ask, "What number is this?" don't tell them. Ask them what number they are calling. If it isn't yours, just say that they have the wrong number. Don't reveal your number to them.

Don't get into a conversation with a prank caller. If someone calls and is playing a prank or saying things that upset you, just hang up. If they keep calling back, stop answering the phone. If the caller should threaten or scare you, call a neighbor or relative and ask if they will come stay with you until an adult comes home.

You might even ask your parents or guardians to get an answering machine. That way, you can screen incoming calls. If it's someone you know leaving a message, you can pick up the phone and speak with them.

In addition, always have a list of emergency numbers handy. This list should include the police, the fire department, your parents' or guardians' work numbers, and the numbers of several neighbors and/or relatives. If your community has a 911 service for emergencies, make sure you know how to use it. The telephone can be a lifeline when you're home alone as long as you follow a few easy rules.

Latchkey kids often have to make another decision. What if someone comes to the door when you're home alone? Do not open the door. Never let anyone you do not know into your home. Period. No exceptions. Even if it appears to be a delivery person or a repair person. No one is allowed in unless an adult is there. This includes people who ask to use the telephone or even the bathroom. No exceptions.

What if a stranger comes to the door and says there has been an accident and someone needs help? You still *do not* open the door. Tell him you will call 911 or another emergency number. But do not let him into the house. Although you want to be helpful, you have to think of safety first.

STRANGE NOISES AND WEATHER EMERGENCIES

What if you are home alone and you begin to hear noises in the house that you can't explain? This can be very frightening to a young person. Old houses sometimes creak and settle. Sometimes an animal can get into a basement or attic. But if you can't explain the noise and think someone may be in the house, then call for help. Call a neighbor who could come over and take you to their house until your parents or guardians get home. If you are sure there is a person in the house, then get out quickly and run to a neighbor for help. Call the police from there, not from your house before you leave.

If you think someone might be trying to break in to the

*Taking care of yourself
after school is one thing.
Taking care of younger brothers
and sisters adds an extra layer
of responsibility.*

house, don't leave. Call 911 and have the police come as quickly as they can. Stay on the phone with the 911 operator until the police arrive.

If you are home alone and it begins to look very dark and threatening outside, try to get a weather report on the radio or television. You and your family will have plenty of warning if a hurricane or blizzard is due in your area. But other storms come up quickly, particularly summer storms, which may bring heavy rain, lightning, and thunder.

If there is a very bad storm approaching your area or the possibility of one, call your parents or guardians. Perhaps they can come home early. Or you might ask to go to a neighbor's until the storm passes. If you do leave the house, make sure all the windows are closed and the doors locked when you leave. And don't forget your keys!

Of course, if a storm has already hit, you'll be safest riding it out at home. Don't even consider leaving the house to go to a neighbor's.

With the number of latchkey kids increasing every year, there are now organizations offering programs designed to help kids become more confident and self-reliant at an early age. Many of these are run through the schools. If you do become a latchkey kid, you'll be better equipped to handle it if you have enrolled in one of these programs. In fact, any kind of program that gives kids more confidence in themselves is a good thing, whether they become latchkey kids or not!

Some communities now have latchkey hotlines, phone numbers that kids can call if they need help or if they just want someone to talk with or to reassure them. In some towns this hotline is called "Phone Friend." People answering the hotline phones are trained to help with everything from setting an oven to the proper temperature to dealing with power outages after a storm. They will also just chat with you if you're lonely or frightened.

If your community does not have a latchkey hotline, you might suggest that your parents or guardians get together with the families of other latchkey kids and start one. If it does have a hotline, the number will be listed in the phone book. Make sure you know how to find it, and don't be afraid to use it. The hotline is there to make your life as a latchkey kid more comfortable, secure, and safe.

It's never easy to predict what is going to happen in the world outside your home. That's why parents today must help prepare their kids by making them aware of the dangers they might face. Keeping children sheltered from the real world doesn't work anymore. Being aware of danger is the first step toward avoiding it.

Young people must also prepare themselves for what they may encounter on the streets, at school, on buses and trains, at shopping malls and rock concerts, or when they are at home alone. The more knowledge you have about potential dangers, the less fear you'll have. You will also be better prepared to avoid traps and deal with any emergencies that might arise.

This book is designed to help. Parents, guardians, teachers, law enforcement officials, clergy, and community leaders can all assist you in your efforts to stay safe when you're on your own. Safety is a total group effort. For the more you know about what to expect and how to handle it, the safer you will be.

FURTHER READING

Brown, Gene. *Violence on America's Streets*. Brookfield, Conn.: Millbrook, 1992.

Goedecke, Christopher J. *Smart Moves: A Kid's Guide to Self-Defense*. New York: Simon & Schuster, 1995.

Goldentyer, Debra. *Gangs*. Austin, Tex.: Steck-Vaughn, 1993.

Guernsey, Joann B. *Sexual Harassment: A Question of Power*. Minneapolis: Lerner, 1995.

Kasdin, Karin, and Laura Szabo-Cohen. *Being Home Alone: A Kid's Guide to Becoming a Disaster Blaster*. New York: Avon, 1995.

Kyte, Kathy. *Play It Safe: The Kid's Guide to Personal Safety and Crime Prevention*. New York: Knopf, 1983.

Long, Lynette, and Thomas Long. *The Handbook for Latchkey Children and Their Parents*. New York: Arbor, 1983.

Miller, Maryann. *Coping with Weapons and Violence in School and on Your Streets*. New York: Rosen, 1993.

Palmer, Jed. *Everything You Need to Know When You Are the Victim of a Violent Crime*. New York: Rosen, 1988.

Terrell, Ruth H. *A Kid's Guide to How to Stop the Violence*. New York: Avon, 1992.

ORGANIZATIONS
TO CONTACT

National Child Safety Council
(They send their materials to local police departments. This material can be obtained by calling liaison officers or D.A.R.E. participating officers in your community. The material includes games and puzzles that help kids deal with problems such as stranger-danger.)

National Clearinghouse for Alcohol and Drug Information
P.O. Box 2345
Rockville, MD 20847
1-800-729-6686
(This organization provides all kinds of pamphlets, brochures, posters, video- and audiotapes, and books. The majority are free, but there may be a charge for some videos or video-book combinations.)

National McGruff House Network
66 East Cleveland Avenue
Salt Lake City, UT 84115
1-800-486-8768
(Find out if McGruff Houses and McGruff Truck programs exist in your area, and how to start them if they don't.)

National Missing Child Hotline
1-800-I AM LOST

National Organization for Victim Assistance (NOVA)
1757 Park Rd. NW
Washington, DC 20010
1-202-232-6682
(This group furnishes a variety of pamphlets regarding sexual assault and other forms of physical abuse, plus crisis information on dealing with being a victim of violence. The material is free for victims.)

National Safe Kids Campaign
111 Michigan Avenue NW
Washington, DC 20010-2970
1-202-939-4993
(Ask for a free checklist of tips on traffic safety and other safety issues.)

National Safety Council
444 N. Michigan Avenue
Chicago, IL 60611
1-708-285-1121
(A complete school bus safety program, with videos, literature, and classroom participation is available. It must be ordered by your teacher or your school.)

INDEX

PHOTO CREDITS

Cover photo by Phyllis Picardi/The Picture Cube, Inc.; pp. 6, 11, 33: © Bob Daemmrich/Stock•Boston; pp. 18, 20, 58: © Tony Freeman/PhotoEdit; pp. 40, 63: © Michael Newman/PhotoEdit; p. 42: © David Young-Wolff/PhotoEdit; p. 54: © D&I MacDonald/The Picture Cube, Inc.; p. 65: © Leland Bobbe/Tony Stone Images; p. 74: © Mary Kate Denny/PhotoEdit.